BEE A PARTICULAR OTTER

by

Daphne Neville

Daphne Neville

This second edition is dedicated to Mr Bee.
Mr Bee now lives with Bee and stars with her in such television programmes as "A Day in The Life of The Otter" (BBC TV)

Published by PWS, St. Marys Mills, Chalford,
Nr. Stroud, Gloucestershire. Tel: 028 576 234
Printed by M.R.M. Print of Reading
Illustrated by Jacquie Govier
ISBN 0 907 537 01 4
2nd edition 1986.

INTRODUCING BEE

"Bee" is a small Malaysian otter. She was born in August 1980. She has an endearing little face, wide-set brown eyes and a 'prehistoric' body perfectly designed for both land and water. Each day I look at Bee and I remember how lucky it was that she came to be part of my family.

We were persuaded to buy Bee by Ian Hunter-Darling who is very concerned about the disappearance of the wild otters here in England. There are now only a few hundred otters surviving in the whole of the English and Welsh countryside which makes them nearly extinct. The British otter is a much larger animal than Bee – more the size of a fox – but Ian thought that a little portable otter like Bee would be ideal to take around to show people how beautiful and intelligent all otters are. Otters must be encouraged to live freely and in greater numbers in our countryside. We rashly agreed to try and help.

Bee's mother and father live in a Children's Zoo not far from London. We knew that they had three eleven week old female cubs. We were very nervous as we set off with a cat-basket in the car. I had never seen an otter before.

In the kitchen of the zoo owner's house was a wire cage and inside this cage peeped that little round face with shining, inquisitive eyes. "She's never been handled", said the zoo-keeper, "and her teeth are already very sharp. You'll need tough leather gloves."

My heart sank. Would we ever manage to tame this wild little creature and would we ever manage, all of us, to live together? Well these are some of the TRUE adventures of BEE a most PARTICULAR OTTER.........

BEE'S IN THE BED

My family and I live in a sixteenth century mill in the Cotswolds. It would be a very different life for a small otter from a zoo.

As Bee was so tiny – she was only just weaned at eleven weeks old – it was important that she lived with us in the warm house and we had partitioned off a corner of the children's playroom. We lined the floor with newspaper, placed a large cardboard box full of woollen blankets in the corner and – most necessary for an otter – we gave her a 'pond' in the shape of a washing-up bowl. The zoo-keeper had told me that she liked several kinds of fish so I bought some trout which I carefully filleted and chopped up with a little milk. I also asked the butcher for plenty of fresh minced beef and chicken. She had to have at least three meals a day.

Poor little Bee was very frightened when we opened her travelling basket in her new home. When you have a kitten or a puppy you can cuddle it to settle it in, but you certainly cannot cuddle a wild wriggling object with needle-sharp teeth. She cautiously crept out of the basket and ate her food greedily and then snuggled thankfully into her box of blankets. How long would it take her to trust us? Only time would tell.

My daughter Mary-Dieu, who was then nine, also slept in the playroom. I did not know but each morning – before it was light – Mary-Dieu would creep into Bee's run and sit with her. Otters are nocturnal by nature (we could always hear Bee playing with her toys at night) so getting used to each other in the darkness was, as it turned out, the very best of ideas. After about three weeks Bee allowed Mary-Dieu to stroke her and before we realized it, Bee had decided that we were all right and that the bed was definitely her property. She abandoned her run, jumped into the bed and Mary-Dieu had to move to the bedroom next door!

Bee was now all set to take over the entire house. Something would most certainly have to be done!!

CLARA'S NEW CLOTHES

By the time Bee was six months old and the weather was warmer we had a very big run put up in the garden. It has its own stream flowing through it and our rabbit-hutch packed with straw converted into excellent sleeping quarters for her. She needs a healthy outdoor life with plenty of space – indoors will only do for very small otters.

Although Bee was over-joyed by her run she naturally missed the house and she was very pleased indeed when her friend Clara (it is Clara's Mother who has drawn the pictures in this book) invited her to stay. It was just before the school term and Clara took Bee upstairs to admire her new uniform which was neatly laid out on the bed. Well, as you very well know, Bee just loves beds and soon she was wriggling in and out of the bedclothes just like she does at home. It is very natural for otters to wriggle through things as in the wild they need to squeeze through the reeds and grasses near their 'holts' where they rest in order to dry their wet coats. Soon Bee was also wriggling into the arms of Clara's new cardigan and it was great fun to play with her shoes, to throw them up by their laces and to roll them under the carpet. Quite quickly even Clara thought this might be too much of a joke – you could hardly see any floor for the scattered clothes. She went downstairs to fetch her Mother but when they arrived back in the bedroom there was no Bee. They searched and they called. They looked in the bathroom, the other bedrooms and downstairs again, but no Bee. All the windows and doors were shut ... "She's just vanished", sobbed Clara. "We'll never see her again."

"Better tidy up and get your books ready for school", said her Mother. "She'll turn up. She must." Clara collected her pencils and her felt-tips, she found her holiday library books and her ruler – but where was her satchel to put them all into? There hanging in the corner! She went to fetch it. It felt very heavy. It started to wriggle! And inside, of course, was Bee. All curled up and waiting. She wanted to go off to school too!

RULES

THE MAGNOLIA BATHROOM

As it happened Bee did not have to wait very long to go to school. Once she became tame it seemed that everyone wanted to meet her. She was photographed for all the local and many of the national newspapers and she appeared on television, sometimes with her friend Spike Milligan. The hoped for invitations to visit schools soon rolled in.

The very first school to invite her was Hatherop Castle. This is a girls' Boarding School set in beautiful grounds near Cirencester. Bee, Ian and I were ushered into the Library where about fifty girls were waiting for us. I held Bee and Ian – the otter expert – told the girls about otters – how there are nineteen different species of otter and how they live in all the countries of the world except for Australia, New Zealand, the island of Madagascar and the Artic and the Antarctic. In Brazil, for instance, the otters are 9ft – 2.7 metres long. He told them of plans to breed young European otters for release into our countryside.

All the girls wanted to know why Bee is called 'Bee'. "It's short, she's as busy as a bee and, because she is a member of the mustalid family like the stoat and the badger with a scent gland by her tail, she smells of honey. Also there is a loch in Scotland – where luckily otters are more plentiful – called Loch Bee.

Very soon Bee became restless and rather hot. Knowing her love of water (the Greek word for an otter is 'Lutra Lutra' which means 'water'). I asked if she could have a swim in a bath like at home. "Of course", replied the Headmistress. "I think the Magnolia bathroom would do nicely." So the school matron was called for and soon Bee was swimming up and down in a large old-fashioned bath. The girls queued up excitedly in the corridor and were allowed in two at a time. They brought her a little toy duck and she peeped up at them from the edge of the bath. Then she swished back into the water using her strong tail just like the rudder of a boat. The girls continued to come in two by two and Bee continued her wonderful swim. Everyone got soaking wet and everyone loved it. And after her swim? A good rub dry in a fluffy towel and tea and madeira cake in the Headmistress' study. Bee felt really quite grown-up. She may even consider an otter 'O' level!

ORIENTAL TWINS

It is not, perhaps, remarkable that Bee and my daughter Mary-Dieu are such good friends. After all they have a great deal in common.

They are both from the East of the World: Bee's parents are from Malaysia and Mary-Dieu was born in Vietnam and rescued from the bitter fighting out there when she was nearly four years old.

Bee and Mary-Dieu are very much the same 'age'. Bee is now two years old but an otter's age can be multiplied by six in human terms. We hope that Bee will live until she is at least twelve.

MOST OF ALL MARY-DIEU AND BEE LOVE WATER. As soon as she gets home from school (except in really wintry weather) Mary-Dieu changes into her swimming costume, lets Bee out of her run and together they dive into the lake. Neither of them ever seems to feel the cold as it is very cold water indeed. Like all otters Bee has two layers of fur – the inside layer keeps her dry. Mary-Dieu is decidedly plump so she keeps warm that way.

Of course otters are better designed than humans for swimming. Their bodies are stream-lined and their heads are like flat pebbles. Their eyes, which they keep open under water, are set high in their heads so that they can see over the surface. Their ears and their nostrils have little valves to keep the water out but unlike many water animals otters frequently need to keep coming up for air.

For a small girl Mary-Dieu swims quite fast but not as fast as Bee. Otters can swim at up to twelve miles an hour.

Otters also enjoy themselves all day long. Bee and Mary-Dieu chase each other, they search for minnows and frogs and they dive right down to the bottom of the lake twisting and turning somersaults. Mary-Dieu and Bee are quite simply WATER-BABIES.

BEE JOINS THE ARMY

When Bee was all of eight months old she was asked to join the Army – for a fund-raising Concert. She consulted with the Commanding Officer of the Royal Corps of Transport at South Cerney, near Cirencester, in his office over a saucer of coffee. It was arranged that we would stage a Grand Variety Show and that Bee would entertain the children in the interval. Top of the Bill in the Variety Show was to be Julian Slade who wrote the famous Musical "Salad Days".

Julian and his Mother are neighbours of ours and one day he telephoned to say that they would like to meet Bee before the Concert and would she please come over to Tea. Bee was delighted with the macaroons and she had never tasted china tea before. She explored the sitting-room with its chintzy chair-covers and then cuddled up to Mrs. Slade like an old friend. Quite suddenly she decided to leap on to Julian's piano. What should I do? "She's musical, she loves it", Julian exclaimed. "Let's see how she likes **my** music." "It is quite obvious", Julian stated after a few minutes. "It is quite obvious who will top the bill at the Show. Bee has star-quality. She will sing at our Concert."

Eight-hundred and fifty people sat in the huge Army Hall. Eight-hundred and fifty pairs of eyes watched spell-bound as Julian Slade sang his own songs at the especially tuned piano on the stage. Also watching was the entire band of the Royal Corps of Transport. Bee waited on my shoulder in the wings. Would she know what to do? Would she do nothing and make a fool of us all? Would she escape? The music changed to "Look at me, I'm Dancing". It was her cue. Bee's little nose twitched and she started to tune up.

Now, otters have very highly pitched voices designed by nature to carry long distances along the water. This is so that otter cubs in their holts can be heard a long way off by their mother when she is out fishing. Bee's voice is no exception. The song ended and we stepped up on to the stage. We stood by Julian at the piano and Bee faced the microphone. And did she sing? Of course she did. "It's EASY to Sing a Simple Song if you sing it after ....BEE EE......."

A GHOST AT BERKELEY CASTLE

One of the next places which we visited for "Outward Bound" was Berkeley Castle by the River Severn. It is the oldest castle to be lived in by one family and Bee felt very honoured to be introduced to Mr. John Berkeley himself. As usual with people she likes she leapt on to his shoulder and then 'interviewed' him in his private library. After this interview and a taste of sherry the Chief Guide arrived and we were all set to be shown over the Castle.

Back on my shoulder and chattering away in her 'birdlike' fashion Bee's voice echoed along the stone passages and staircases. We inspected the dungeon where poor King Edward II met his horrible death and then moved towards a large hall filled with armoury. A party of American tourists were there. This was too much for Bee. She jumped off my shoulder on to a chair and literally vanished.

Not wanting to alarm the tourists I tried to keep very calm. I searched high and low looking behind the heavy tapestries and even into the priceless Chinese vases. Luckily no one else knew anything had gone wrong. I was desperately anxious that Bee had not gone back to look down the dark hole to the dungeon. Even if she survived the drop how would we get her out? Suddenly there was a shriek, "Elmer, there's a GHOST, the armour, its moving!" All the Americans stood transfixed as the vizor on the helmet of a suit of armour moved up and down, first very slowly and then quite fast. "Oh, Elmer", repeated the lady faintly. Quite suddenly, the vizor opened and out popped a little brown head.

Bee's eyes blinked in astonishment as the tourists' cameras clicked and even Elmer's wife mopped her brow, patted her curls and exclaimed, "Why Elmer, that's the strangest 'ghost' I ever did see." And Bee? She wasn't too worried. Ghost or no ghost she's in the entertainment business and there the unexpected always hits the headlines. And if her larger otter 'cousins' in America should ever benefit from the efforts of their small Public Relations Otter in little old England, why so much the better.

A FISHY TAIL

The furthest distance that Bee has herself travelled for "Outward Bound" was up to Bewdley in Worcestershire to the West Midland Safari Park there.

Bee was as fascinated as I was to be driven through the great enclosures of lions and giraffes, to see the monkeys clamber on to the bonnet of the car and we even stopped and climbed up a huge observation tower. It was just like being in Africa.

I knew from books that otters are thought to have lived in the world for as many as one hundred thousand years and that they are probably the oldest aquatic mammal – even older in history than the whale and the sea-lion. But as Bee had never met a sea-lion I could only use my imagination.

Now we were being led into the sea-lion enclosure and were treated to an incredible display of trust and intelligence between the trainer and the two animals. When the public had gone I asked if Bee could meet the sea-lions face to face. They were so huge compared with her – she is after all only the size of a very small cat. The large dewy eyes of the sea-lions shone in recognition of their smaller guest and a fish was offered and accepted. Very soon three 'pre-historic' tails were flashing through the blue water.

The sea-lions' trainer was astonished. "Please will you let Bee join our act permanently?", he pleaded. I was dumbfounded. Here was a sight maybe no one else in the whole world had ever seen. Millions of people would be able to see how an otter behaves (not just the comparitively few Bee meets as schools). Bee would certainly be happy – they were kind people and the sea-lions loved her – of that there was no doubt at all **but** life without Bee would be unthinkable. Who would unmake the beds and who would stir the eggs for breakfast? Who would 'keep us on our toes' from morning to night? Was I being selfish? Would Bee really be happier with her own kind? My thoughts raced ahead and then they were over. For a little wet body crawled out of the pool and into my arms. "Time to go HOME", Bee said.

BEE MAKES AN OMELETTE

Please do not think that otters make ideal pets. They are full of fun but they are as mischievous as any monkey, they need round-the-clock attention and they would soon drive an average family completely mad! Here's another true story to prove it:

As Bee was brought up in the house she considers this her right and proper place to be. She seizes every opportunity to get there escaping from her beautiful run with its rushing stream whenever she can. Even when she takes her twice-daily swim in our lake she quickly shakes herself dry and darts to the kitchen door which she knows how to open as well as any burglar.

One day I was out for the morning and Bee did this burglary act. She sneaked into the kitchen and literally made a 'bee-line' for the kitchen cupboard where she knows I keep the eggs. By lying on the floor and working away with her paws (she has stubby little ones unlike the long-clawed English otter) she forced the magnetic catch to open. Then she carefully carried a large egg to the kitchen floor, banged it on the ground, broke it and – letting all the yoke and egg-white spill away – she gleefully crunched up the shell. This she repeated another eleven times until all the dozen egg-shells were used up. Then calling Daisy-May our Airedale puppy over from her basket, she stirred up all the eggs giving Daisy a delicious treat for her lunch. Daisy was just gobbling down the last of the omelette as I arrived back with the shopping. Bee even had the nerve to climb into my shopping basket to see if she could find any more eggs! As for Daisy-May she slept very deeply that afternoon dreaming no doubt of the best meal she'd ever eaten.

BEE GOES TO THE SEASIDE

When she is at home Bee swims at least twice a day in our lake and in the river nosing around for small fish like 'bull-heads' and tiddlers which she catches and gobbles up quickly. However she had always swum in fresh and never in salt water. One evening I was watching a beautiful film about sea-otters in Scotland and I wondered how Bee would herself take to the sea.

The chance came when we had a few days holiday in Dorset. We parked our car near some sand-dunes and taking a flask of fresh water with us – just in case she got thirsty – we all ran down the path to the SEA.

Bee could not believe her eyes. There was so much exciting sand to dig into and the water seemed to be playing 'tag' with her.

She was a bit nervous at first and kept 'testing' the water just like an old grandmother. Then she found a little rock pool and dived in flashing out again with a large shrimp. She was in ecstasy. Far from distressing her the salt water seemed to suit her and the seaweed was a paradise for a small otter to explore.

Just as Bee was finding her 'sea-legs' in the pool there was a bark from along the beach and up bounded an enormous brown dog whose owner called after him, "Spring, come here boy. Spring". 'Spring' took absolutely no notice of the command and bounced over to Bee, determined to chase out this intruder on **his** beach. Bee, being quite used to dogs and well practised in controlling our Daisy-May, simply nipped his ear and squeaked, "Go Away." Spring was terrified – he decided to clear-off before this small monster attacked him again. But where should he go? "The sea – I'll be quite safe in all those waves. No object such as this could catch me out there", he decided. Poor Spring – I bet you can guess what happened .... No sooner had he waded out than the torpedo struck. Down into the waves Bee dived and up again just behind that dog. And just as his tail was starting to wag with relief it was grabbed and bitten extremely hard. Poor Spring, he just SPRANG, and I do not think that his seaside visits will be quite the same ever again!

BEE 100

BEE'S BRUSH WITH THE LAW

Bee is used to travelling in the back of my car in a large wire cage. She loves this cage as it means an adventure with plenty of people to admire her and when I get it ready for a journey with a special towel folded in it and a dish of food she leaps inside with a tremendous jump.

On one of our journeys on the way to visit a school, I stopped the car on a yellow line and hurried into a shop to collect some groceries, having opened the hatch-back of the car so that I could put them in quickly. As I returned with a cardboard box in my arms, I was horrified to see that an enormous crowd had gathered around the car and that the road was quite blocked with people. Bee of course loves an audience and had decided to squeak "Hello" to all the passers-by, most of whom had never seen, let alone heard, an otter before.

Just as I was easing my way through this crowd a large policeman appeared from the market stalls. "'Ere, 'ere, what's all this – causing a public disturbance, are we, Madam?" "I'm so sorry, Officer", I muttered. "We didn't mean to. It's just that my otter must have...", he cut me short. "Your otter, Madam? You mean your otter, Bee?" "Why yes, Officer, do you know her?" "Know her, know her? Of course I know her – my kids and I saw her yesterday afternoon on the tele. Tell you what, Madam", he said, winking at the crowd. "If her and you come along and open our fete next June, we'll er ... say no more about this little episode. And you", he beamed at the crowd, "You will all be most welcome to come."

"Special Attractions" read the poster ..."Hot-air ballooning & Bee the otter".

The crowds did come and our friendly policeman made a welcoming speech. Bee squeaked a "reply", the band played her favourite tune – "The Yellow Submarine" and that was how Bee officially, and extremely legally, declared her first fete OPEN.

BEE
'THE OTTER'

BEE EARNS HER BLUE PETER BADGE

One of the Television Programmes our friend the policeman might have seen Bee on was Blue Peter. Bee was very proud when she drove to the BBC Television Centre in London and her round brown eyes shone with glee when she looked at her Dressing Room door with "BEE THE OTTER" and a yellow star underneath it! Inside the room was a couch, a mirror framed with lights and best of all – her very own wash hand-basin. She had a quick splash around as it gets very hot travelling in a car if you are an otter. She also wanted to look spick and span for her big moment.....

Just as Bee was having a final soak a most familiar face popped round the door. It was one of the Japanese stars of a television serial called 'Tenko' who she had met on her seaside holiday in Dorset. He was now filming some studio shots and had the dressing-room next door.

After the lunch-break Bee was taken to the Blue Peter Studio where she met Sarah, who was to conduct the interview along with wild-life expert George Cansdale. She also met Simon and Peter and, of course, Goldie the retriever. A special blue bath complete with running taps had been installed in the studio for her to swim in.

Bee was to be the 'star-turn' at the end of the programme and suddenly there she was being lifted into George Cansdale's arms. She sat very still while he explained about otters all over the world and their fight to survive in waters often polluted with pesticides and fertilizers. He hoped that river authorities would be more aware of the otter's need for reeds and tree-stumps to live in.

Bee had been admiring Sarah's earrings very much and with a little leap she sprang on to Sarah's shoulder to inspect them. Then she dived into the blue bath. Goldie came over to look and Sarah just managed to stop Bee from following her. Bee played with the ping-pong balls floating on the water and took no notice of the cameras zooming in close. After all she was enjoying herself with plenty of friends. It was really just like her playtime at home.